No-Code Automation and Programming Strategies

About The Author

I was born in Madrid in 1975. Since I was a child I have been passionate about computers and new technologies. I started my journey programming nonsense on a Commodore VIC20.

I am a computer scientist by study, a profession and it is my hobby. I enjoy systems, networks, computing, and all things technology. If we had to define the work I do on a daily basis, it would be *a Systems Architect, specializing in data center services*.

I started working as an employee in Spain in services related to the stock market. At that moment I realized the importance of data centers, high availability, efficient network management and above all data accessibility and security.

In 2006 the idea for my company was born and in 2010, I founded IT Encore. Company specialized in offering data center, disaster recovery and infrastructure management services.

In the year 2024-2025, which is when this book is being written, we operate in 3 data centers in Spain and two in Europe, for contingency services. With over 1,000 virtual machines running.

The idea of automation is an obsession I've had since I started installing my first computer. And why, if I repeat all this so many times, will there be no way to automate it?

And from here, everything I repeat twice, I try to automate it. This has always saved me a lot of time, both for me and for my clients.

I am currently also working on projects related to remote virtual desktops, data center automation and infrastructure software management (IaaS).

Mr. Jaime Rodríguez Molina

Collaborations and Co-authors

Dr. Alberto Rodríguez Molina

Professor of Acoustics and Audiovisual Music at the International University of La Rioja. It studies the integration of New Technologies, based on computers and electronics, and Artificial Intelligence in musical composition and sound design oriented to Foley ambience and soundscape through programming in MAX-MSP, SuperCollider, Wwise, FMOD Studio, etc.

He is co-founder of the record label CMYBaroque for which he works as a Music Producer and Editor. In this field he has also worked as a sound technician for the record labels Brilliant and Panclassics.

Much of his work is developed in the pedagogy of music and sound applied to Musical Composition.

Content

Chapter 1

Introduction to no-code automation

What is automation?

Automation refers to the use of technologies and tools that allow tasks and processes to be executed automatically, reducing or eliminating human intervention.

In the context of social networks and digital marketing, automation has become a key solution to optimize time and resources, since content generation is very tedious.

It allows users to manage multiple activities, from content publishing to data analysis, without the need for programming or software development skills.

Thanks to automation, companies can focus on more strategic and creative activities, leaving repetitive tasks to technology.

There are a variety of platforms and services that make it easy to automate processes without coding. These no-code tools allow users to create custom workflows using intuitive and user-friendly interfaces.

For example, applications such as Zapier *(https://zapier.com)*, Make *(https://make.com)* (formerly Integromat) or n8n (https://n8n.io), allow different tools and applications to be integrated, making them work together automatically. This means that if a task is completed in one application, another action can be triggered in a different application, all without the user having to write a single line of code. To integrate these actions, a connector called an API is used.

In the field of digital marketing, automation is used to schedule social media posts, manage email campaigns, and analyze the performance of implemented strategies.

Automation tools can help segment audiences and personalize messages, which improves the effectiveness of campaigns. By automating these tasks, marketers can focus on creating quality content and developing new strategies that attract and retain customers.

The creation of **chatbots** is another example of how automation is transforming the way businesses interact with their customers.

Without the need for programming knowledge, it is possible to develop chatbots that answer frequently asked questions, make bookings, or even complete online sales. These chatbots improve the user experience by providing quick and accurate responses, which also frees up time for customer service teams to focus on resolving more complex issues.

Finally, **automating reporting and data analytics** allows businesses to make informed decisions based on real-time metrics and results. Tools that integrate ecommerce platforms, manage business workflows, and create forms and surveys, make accessing relevant information easier and more efficient.

By adopting automation, organizations not only optimize their day-to-day operations, but also better position themselves in a competitive environment that demands speed and adaptability.

Benefits of automation in business

Although the title says it all and seems obvious, automation in business has transformed the way companies operate, allowing for a more efficient and effective approach to their processes. One of the most prominent benefits of automation is the reduction of time on repetitive tasks.

By implementing tools that allow processes such as social media management or reporting to be automated, companies can free up valuable time that can be allocated to more strategic and creative activities. Not only does this improve productivity, but it also allows teams to focus on growth and innovation.

Another important aspect of automation is the minimization of human error. By using no-code solutions for building applications or automating workflows, you can ensure greater accuracy in the tasks performed.

For example, in the integration of ecommerce platforms, automation helps to manage inventories and orders more skillfully, reducing the potential complications that can arise from manual intervention. This translates into a better customer experience and higher overall satisfaction.

Automation also boosts data analysis capabilities. By using tools that enable reporting and analysis automation, businesses can gain valuable insights quickly and efficiently. This allows them to make decisions based on hard data, rather than relying on assumptions. The ability to generate digital marketing performance analysis or manage surveys without code becomes a key resource to adjust strategies and improve results.

In addition, automation makes it easy to integrate various productivity tools. Many businesses use multiple applications and platforms to conduct their daily operations. Automation allows these tools to be connected seamlessly, optimizing the flow of information and reducing the need for manual changes between systems. Not only does this simplify management, but it also improves collaboration between teams, ensuring everyone is on the same page and working towards the same goals.

Finally, automation offers a significant competitive advantage in an increasingly dynamic business environment. Companies that adopt automated solutions can adapt more quickly to changes in the market and respond effectively to customer needs. This translates into greater agility and ability to innovate, which is crucial for long-term success. By taking advantage of the opportunities offered by automation, companies not only improve their operational efficiency, but also position themselves favorably against the competition.

The rise of no-code tools

The term "**no-code**" refers to a development and automation approach that allows people to create applications, websites, workflows, and other digital processes without needing to write traditional programming code. Rather than requiring specialized technical expertise, no-code platforms offer intuitive visual interfaces with drag-and-drop functionalities, pre-built templates, and pre-configured connectors that allow users with no programming experience to create functional digital solutions.

This approach democratizes technological development, allowing marketing professionals, entrepreneurs, designers, and other non-technical profiles to implement their ideas and automate processes without relying on professional developers or programmers. No-code tools have revolutionized fields such as web development, marketing automation, data management, and mobile app creation, making digital transformation more accessible to everyone.

The rise of no-code tools has transformed the way people and businesses approach process automation. These tools allow users to create applications, workflows, and digital solutions without the need for programming skills. In a world where agility and efficiency are crucial, no-code is presented as an accessible solution for those who want to optimize their operations without relying on an extensive technical team.

In the field of digital marketing, no-code platforms have made it easier to create and manage automated campaigns. Users can design sales funnels, manage emails, and analyze performance data without writing a single line of code. This democratizes access to advanced tools, allowing entrepreneurs and small businesses to compete on equal terms with large corporations that have significant technological resources.

Mobile app creation has also been revolutionized by the no-code movement. Nowadays, anyone with an idea can develop a functional and attractive app through intuitive platforms that offer templates and drag-and-drop functionalities. Not only does this save time and money, but it also encourages innovation, as more people can bring their ideas to market without facing traditional barriers to development.

The integration of productivity tools is another field where no-code has gained ground. With the ability to connect different applications and services, users can automate workflows, reduce repetitive tasks, and improve team collaboration. For example, it is possible to synchronize calendars, manage projects and share documents automatically, which optimizes time and minimizes human errors.

Finally, chatbot development and social media management automation are clear examples of how no-code has simplified complex processes. These tools allow companies to interact with their customers in an efficient and personalized way, without the need for specialized developers. In short, the rise of no-code tools represents an unprecedented opportunity for anyone, regardless of their technical level, to participate in the creation and automation of solutions that improve their productivity and effectiveness in the digital environment.

Chapter 2

No-Code Service Automation

Popular Tools on the Market

In the world of automation, there are various tools that allow users to optimize processes and improve their productivity without the need for programming knowledge. Designed to be intuitive and accessible, these tools are ideal for those looking to simplify their daily tasks and make the most of the possibilities offered by technology. Among the most popular are Zapier, Integromat, and Airtable, each with unique features to suit different needs.

Zapier (*https://zapier.com*) is one of the most recognized platforms for workflow automation. It allows more than two thousand applications to be connected, facilitating the transfer of information between them without manual intervention. For example, you can set up a "zap" so that every time you receive an email with an attachment, it is automatically saved to Google Drive. Its interface is user-friendly and requires no technical knowledge, making it an attractive option for anyone who wants to optimize repetitive tasks.

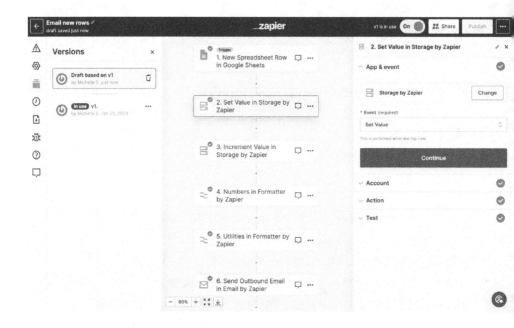

Integromat, now known as **Make** *(https://make.com),* offers a similar experience, but with a more visual and comprehensive approach. Through its visual editor, users can create complex scenarios that integrate multiple applications and functions. This is especially useful for those who want to automate digital marketing processes, such as sending personalized emails based on user actions on a website. Integromat's flexibility allows users to design workflows that are perfectly suited to their specific needs.

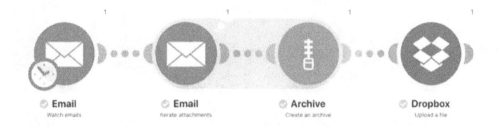

Visualize everything you do

With Integromat's interactive approach and look, you can watch in real-time how your automation is executed and how data flows through your scenario.

Email
Watch emails

Email
Iterate attachments

Archive
Create an archive

Dropbox
Upload a file

N8N *(https://n8n.io)* is a workflow automation tool that allows you to connect different applications and services without the need for programming. You can use n8n in two ways: by installing it locally or using the cloud version. The essential difference from Make or Zapier is that it is *open source*. Its learning curve is perhaps more complex than its competitors. It's the one I'm currently using.

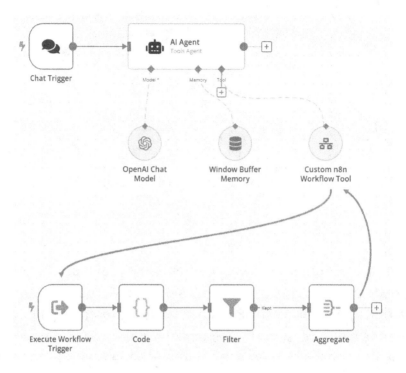

Storage and Database

Airtable, *(https://www.airtable.com)* on the other hand, although not an automation tool as such, combines the functionality of a spreadsheet with that of a database, allowing users to manage projects and collaborate efficiently. Its ability to create no-code forms and surveys makes it easy to collect data and interact with customers.

Tables

In addition, Airtable easily integrates with other automation tools, allowing project management to be done in a smooth and organized manner, without technical complications.

Chatbots

A chatbot is a computer program designed to hold conversations with humans, usually through text, but also by voice, speaking into the microphone of the phone or computer.

Its main characteristics are:

- Use artificial intelligence
- Process natural language
- Understand user questions or comments
- Provide relevant answers
- Answers frequently asked questions
- Help provide customer service or basic technical support
- Perform simple tasks like scheduling appointments
- Provides information about products or services
- Assist in purchasing processes

For those interested in chatbot development, platforms such as Chatfuel (*https://chatfuel.com/*) and ManyChat (*https://maychat.com*) offer practical solutions for the creation of these virtual assistants without the need for programming. These tools allow you to design conversation flows that improve customer service and automate responses to frequently asked questions, saving time and resources.

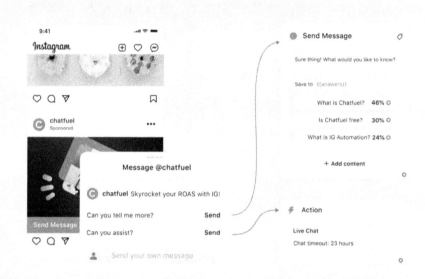

The integration of these platforms with social media and messaging apps has revolutionized the way businesses interact with their users.

Automation tools available on the market give users the opportunity to improve their efficiency and simplify processes without the need to be programming experts.

From app integration, to chatbot development, to form creation, these no-code solutions have become indispensable resources for anyone who wants to get the most out of technology in their personal or professional life.

With the right choice, it's possible to transform the way daily tasks are managed and free up time to focus on what really matters.

Use cases in different industries

Today, process automation has become a fundamental tool in various industries. Through no-code solutions, companies can optimize their operation without the need for a team of highly specialized developers.

For example, in the digital marketing industry, automation platforms allow you to schedule email campaigns, manage social media, and perform data analytics efficiently. This not only saves time, but also improves the effectiveness of the strategies implemented.

In the realm of mobile app building, no-code tools have revolutionized the way businesses can develop their products.

Now, anyone with an idea can create a functional application without knowing how to code. This has democratized access to technology, allowing small businesses and individuals to join the digital marketplace with innovative solutions that previously required large investments in development.

Integrating productivity tools is also a prominent use case across multiple industries. For example, companies of different sizes use platforms that allow applications such as calendars, project management systems, and communication software to be connected.

This facilitates collaboration between teams and improves the operational experience, as response times are reduced and human errors in information transfer are minimized.

Social media management is another area where automation has had a significant impact. Tools that allow you to schedule posts and analyze their performance are essential for any digital marketing strategy.

In addition, the development of no-code chatbots is transforming customer support, as these tools can answer frequently asked questions and provide assistance 24 hours a day, improving the user experience and freeing up time for support teams.

Finally, automating business workflows and creating no-code forms and surveys have enabled organizations to efficiently collect valuable information. This is crucial for informed decision-making.

The integration of e-commerce platforms and the automation of reports and data analysis are also key aspects that help companies quickly adapt to market trends and improve their overall performance. As these technologies continue to evolve, it is evident that their implementation will become increasingly vital to the success of organizations in a competitive environment.

How to Choose the Right Tool

When selecting the right tool for process automation, it's critical to consider the specific needs of your project.

First, evaluate which tasks you want to automate and what the end goal is. For example, if your focus is on social media management, look for tools that offer post scheduling, performance analysis, and auto-response to interactions. Knowing your goals will allow you to filter the options and focus on those that really add value to your strategy.

Another key aspect is the ease of use of the tool. For those who don't possess programming skills, it's crucial to choose platforms that have intuitive interfaces and drag-and-drop options. This will make it easier to deploy and use on a daily basis, eliminating the need for complicated tutorials or constant technical support. Tools such as Zapier, Make or n8n, seen above, are examples of solutions that simplify automation without requiring advanced technical skills.

The tool's compatibility with other platforms is also a determining factor. In a digital environment where multiple applications are used, it is essential that the chosen tool can be easily integrated with your existing systems, such as CRM, email marketing platforms, and social media. Research the available integrations and make sure the tool can connect all elements of your digital ecosystem to streamline workflows.

Also, consider the support and community surrounding the tool. A good option is one that has resources such as tutorials, forums, and accessible customer support. Not only will this help you solve problems quickly, but it will also allow you to learn from other users and improve your use of the tool. Active communities can be a great source of ideas and tricks that make it even easier to automate your processes.

Finally, don't forget to evaluate the cost of the tool in relation to its benefits. Many options offer free or trial versions, allowing you to experiment before committing financially.

Compare the features and prices of various tools to find the one that best suits your budget and needs. Taking the time to research and test different solutions will allow you to choose the right tool to help you automate your processes efficiently and effectively.

Chapter 3

Digital Marketing Automation Strategies

Email automation

Email automation has become an essential tool for businesses and entrepreneurs looking to streamline their digital marketing processes. It's exasperating to wake up in the morning with your inbox full of emails, most of which you don't care about or are identical to yesterday's.

But it is possible, without the need for technical knowledge or programming, to implement strategies that not only save time, but also improve the effectiveness of communication campaigns. Through automation platforms, anyone can create workflows that send emails to prospects and customers at strategic moments, thus increasing the chances of conversion.

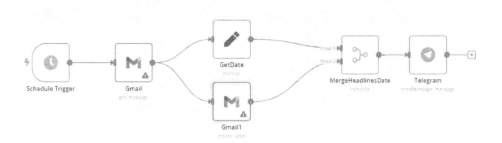

One of the main advantages of email automation is the ability to segment the audience effectively. This is achieved by creating specific lists based on users' previous behavior and interactions.

For example, personalized emails can be sent to those who have shown interest in a particular product or service, resulting in more relevant and personal communication. This segmentation not only improves the relationship with the customer, but also increases the rate of open and clicks on emails.

In addition, automation tools allow you to schedule emails to be sent at optimal times, ensuring that the message arrives in the recipient's inbox at the right time. This is especially useful for campaigns that rely on specific events, such as product launches or special promotions. With good planning, businesses can maximize the impact of their messages and ensure that they are received when users are most likely to engage with them.

No-code form and survey creation also integrates seamlessly with email automation. By capturing valuable information through these forms, contact lists can be nurtured and campaigns can be further personalized. For example, a survey can help identify customer preferences, allowing content specifically designed to meet those needs to be sent. Not only does this improve the user experience, but it also increases brand loyalty and engagement.

Finally, email automation makes it easier to generate reports and analyze data. By monitoring campaign performance, businesses can gain insight into which strategies are working and which ones need adjustments. These analytics are crucial for informed decision-making, allowing you to continuously optimize marketing tactics. In short, email automation is a powerful tool that, without requiring programming skills, offers anyone the opportunity to take their communication and digital marketing to the next level.

No-code segmentation and personalization

No-code segmentation and personalization has become an essential tool for those looking to optimize their digital marketing strategies and improve the user experience. Through no-code platforms and tools, companies can segment their audience effectively, creating specific groups based on demographic, behavioral, and interest criteria. This allows marketers to target their efforts towards the right people, thus increasing the relevance of their messages and the effectiveness of their campaigns.

One of the most significant advantages of no-code targeting is the ease with which changes and adjustments can be implemented. No-code tools allow users to create and modify audience segments without the need for technical knowledge.

For example, platforms such as Zapier or Airtable offer integrations that allow you to collect and analyze data from different sources, making it easier to create segmented lists that are automatically updated. This not only saves time, but also allows for greater agility in responding to market trends.

Personalization is another crucial aspect that benefits from segmentation. By getting to know their audience better, businesses can personalize their messages and offers, increasing the likelihood of conversion. With tools like Mailchimp or HubSpot, users can create email campaigns that are tailored to the preferences and behaviors of each segment. This means that a customer who has shown interest in a specific product will receive relevant and engaging information, which improves the experience and fosters loyalty.

In addition, social media management automation plays an important role in segmentation and personalization. Tools like Buffer *(https://buffer.com)* or Hootsuite *(https://hootsuite.com)* allow users to schedule posts and segment their audience based on previous interactions. Not only does this optimize management time, but it also ensures that the right content reaches the right people at the right time, increasing engagement and effectiveness of social media communication.

Finally, creating forms and surveys without using code also contributes to more effective segmentation. Tools such as Typeform or Google Forms allow you to collect valuable data directly from users, which helps to build more detailed and accurate data. This information can be used to enrich databases and improve the personalization of campaigns, ensuring that marketing strategies are aligned with the needs and preferences of the target audience. Taken together, these no-code segmentation and personalization practices are critical to success in today's digital environment.

Automated social media campaigns

Automated social media campaigns have revolutionized the way businesses and entrepreneurs communicate with their audience. Automation allows multiple platforms to be managed simultaneously, optimizing time and resources. This is especially useful for those who don't have programming skills, as there are tools that make it easy to create and manage campaigns without writing a single line of code. This way, anyone can implement effective strategies that improve their online presence.

One of the main advantages of automated campaigns is the ability to schedule posts at different times and days. This ensures that the content reaches the audience at the most appropriate time, increasing the likelihood of interaction. Likewise, automation tools allow you to track the metrics of each publication, which helps to understand what type of content generates the most interest and *engagement*. These metrics are essential for adjusting strategies in real-time.

In addition, automation makes it easy to integrate various social media platforms. Tools such as Zapier or Male allow you to connect different applications, creating workflows that simplify campaign management. For example, you can automate the posting of content on Facebook every time a new blog post is uploaded, saving time and ensuring that content is shared effectively. This integration also allows businesses to maintain a consistent and consistent presence across multiple platforms.

Another important feature of automated campaigns is the ability to segment the audience. The tools allow messages to be customized according to the user's profile, which increases the relevance of the content. By targeting specific groups, businesses can improve their conversion rate and foster a deeper connection with their followers. Automating segmentation makes this process much more efficient, allowing you to adjust marketing strategies without technical complications.

Finally, automation is not only limited to social media management, but also allows you to create chatbots and interactive forms without the need for coding. This opens up a range of possibilities for interaction with users, facilitating data collection and customer service. Automated campaigns, therefore, not only optimize time and resources, but also create a richer experience for both companies and their customers. Automation is undoubtedly an essential tool for anyone who wants to improve their digital marketing strategy without getting complicated with scheduling.

Chapter 4

No-Code Mobile App Creation

Application Development Platforms

Application development platforms have revolutionized the way individuals and companies create digital solutions, allowing people without programming knowledge to materialize their ideas. These tools, known as "no-code," offer intuitive interfaces that make it easy to design and deploy mobile and web applications. In addition, they make it possible to automate processes that previously required a high level of technical specialization, democratizing access to technology and fostering innovation in various sectors.

One of the main advantages of these platforms is the ability to integrate multiple productivity tools. Users can connect existing apps, such as Google Sheets, Slack, Trello, and more, to streamline their workflows. Not only does this integration improve efficiency, but it also allows for more effective tracking of ongoing tasks and projects. Thus, digital marketers can manage campaigns more effectively, automating the sending of emails, scheduling social media posts, and collecting analytical data.

Chatbot development is another area where no-code platforms shine. These virtual assistants can be created without writing a single line of code, allowing businesses to offer 24/7 customer support and improve the user experience on their websites. Automating social media management is also facilitated through these tools, as they allow you to schedule posts and analyze performance in real-time, which is crucial for optimizing content strategies.

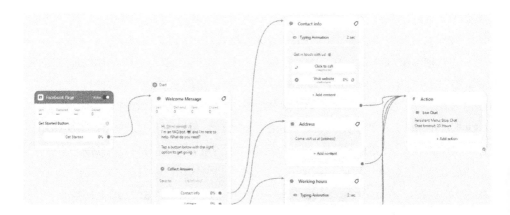

The creation of forms and surveys is equally accessible thanks to these platforms. Users can design custom forms that collect valuable information from customers and prospects without any hassle. This functionality is especially useful for market research and customer feedback. With just a few clicks, it is possible to obtain data that can be analyzed to improve products and services.

Finally, automating reporting and data analysis has become essential for informed decision-making. No-code platforms allow users to generate visual reports and interactive *dashboards* that make it easier to understand key metrics. In addition, the integration of e-commerce platforms with these tools allows entrepreneurs to manage their online stores more efficiently, automating processes such as inventory tracking and order management, thus contributing to a more agile and effective business workflow.

Step-by-step process for creating an app

To create an application without knowing how to code, it is essential to follow a structured process that facilitates automation and the integration of tools. The first step is to define the objective of the application. Ask yourself what problem you want to solve or what specific need you want to meet. This clear approach will help you determine the features and functionality your app should have, as well as the target audience it is aimed at.

Once you're clear on the purpose of your app, the next step is to research and choose the right platform. There are several no-code tools that allow you to create mobile applications without writing code, such as Adalo, Glide or Bubble. These platforms offer an intuitive interface that makes it easy to design and implement the desired functionality. It is advisable to explore the different options and select the one that best suits your needs and knowledge.

The third step is to design the user interface (UI) and user experience (UX). At this stage, you'll need to create a wireframe or simple prototype that shows how your app will look and work. Many no-code tools have pre-designed templates that you can customize.

Make sure the navigation is clear and simple, and the design is attractive to grab users' attention.

Once you have the design ready, it's time to integrate the functionalities you've nested in. This can include creating forms, implementing chatbots, or automating workflows. In this phase, it's crucial to connect the productivity tools you'll be using, such as Google Sheets, Zapier, or Integromat, to automate processes and ensure that information flows properly between the different parts of your app.

Finally, once you've built and tested your app, don't forget the promotion and analytics step. Use social media and other digital marketing platforms to raise awareness of your creation. In addition, set up metrics and analytics tools that allow you to evaluate your app's performance and make adjustments as needed. With this step-by-step process, you will be able to create effective applications without the need for programming knowledge, thus facilitating the automation of your processes and the development of innovative solutions.

Examples of successful applications

One of the most prominent examples of successful applications in the field of process automation is the use of digital marketing tools that require zero programming knowledge. Platforms like Mailchimp and SendinBlue allow businesses to design and send automated email campaigns. Not only do these tools make it easy to segment audiences, but they also allow for the personalization of messages, all without the need to write a single line of code. This has democratized access to digital marketing, allowing small businesses to compete on a level playing field with large corporations.

In the field of mobile app creation, platforms like Adalo and Glide have revolutionized the way entrepreneurs can develop their own apps without coding. Through intuitive interfaces and predefined templates, users can create functional applications that are tailored to their specific needs. These tools are ideal for those who want to bring their idea to market quickly, removing traditional development barriers that often require investment and advanced technical knowledge.

Social media management automation is another field where successful applications have been seen. Tools like Buffer and Hootsuite allow you to schedule posts across multiple platforms, analyze performance, and respond to interactions efficiently. Not only do these solutions save time, but they also maximize the reach and effectiveness of social media campaigns. By offering built-in analytics capabilities, users can adjust their strategies in real-time, improving their results without needing to be network experts.

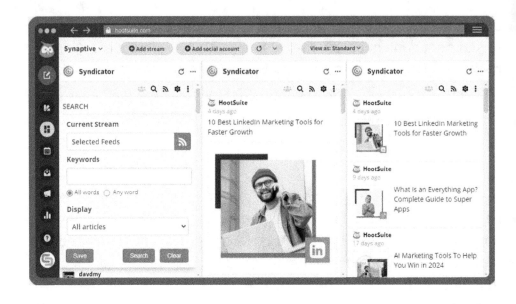

Likewise, the development of chatbots without programming has grown exponentially. Tools like Chatfuel and ManyChat allow businesses to create virtual assistants that interact with customers through platforms like Facebook Messenger. These chatbots can handle common queries, make reservations, or even process orders, improving customer support and freeing up human resources for more complex tasks. The ease of use of these platforms allows anyone, regardless of their technical expertise, to implement a chatbot and improve interaction with their audience.

Finally, the integration of e-commerce platforms has also seen a notable boom in automation. Solutions such as Zapier allow you to connect various applications and automate workflows, facilitating inventory management, sales tracking, and reporting. Not only does this streamline business processes, but it also provides business owners with a clear view of their performance without the need to manually analyze large volumes of data. With these applications, the business landscape becomes more accessible, allowing even those without technical backgrounds to take full advantage of the digital tools available.

Chapter 5

Integration of Productivity Tools

Most Used Productivity Tools

Nowadays, productivity tools have become essential allies for those looking to optimize their time and resources. Especially for those who do not have programming knowledge, there are various platforms that allow you to automate processes in a simple and effective way. These tools are designed to facilitate task management, communication, and collaboration, which is critical in increasingly dynamic and digital work environments.

One of the most widely used tools in the field of digital marketing process automation is Zapier. This platform allows you to connect different applications and automate workflows without writing code. For example, you can set up a zap that, whenever a new contact form is received on a web page, automatically sends a thank you email and records it in a spreadsheet. This integration not only saves time, but also reduces the risk of human error.

Another prominent tool is Airtable, which combines the functionalities of a spreadsheet with a database. It allows users to create custom applications without the need for programming. With Airtable, you can manage projects, track marketing campaigns, and collaborate in real-time with teams, all in one place. Its intuitive interface makes it easy to create forms and organize data, which is especially useful for those looking for an accessible and versatile solution.

In the realm of social media management, tools like Buffer and Hootsuite have gained popularity. These platforms allow you to schedule posts, analyze content performance, and manage multiple accounts from a single dashboard. Automating social media management not only optimizes time, but also helps maintain a consistent and consistent presence across platforms, which is key to success in digital marketing.

Finally, for those interested in creating chatbots, tools like Chatfuel and ManyChat offer effective solutions without the need for technical knowledge. These platforms allow you to design automated conversations that improve customer service and optimize communication on social networks. The automation of business workflows, as well as the generation of reports and data analysis, are significantly benefited by these innovations, allowing companies to make more informed and strategic decisions.

Key integrations for an efficient workflow

Key integrations are critical to optimizing an efficient workflow in process automation. In the context of social networks and digital marketing, these integrations allow you to connect different tools that, although separately useful, when joined together multiply their effectiveness. A clear example is the integration of social media management platforms with data analysis tools. Not only does this make it easier to publish content, but it also allows you to measure the impact of campaigns in real-time, which is essential for proactively adjusting strategies.

Automating business workflows is another critical aspect. By implementing no-code tools, users can create processes that connect apps like Google Sheets, Trello, and Slack without the need for coding. These integrations allow, for example, information entered into a Google Form to be automatically transposed to a

Trello board, assigning tasks to different team members. This eliminates manual steps, reduces errors, and saves valuable time.

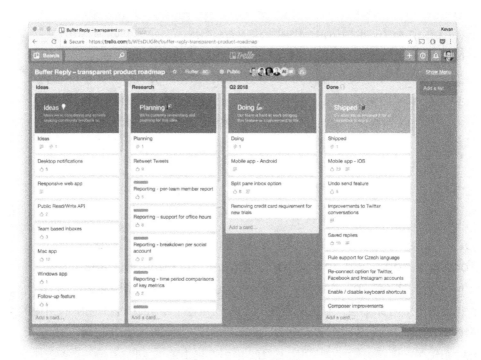

Creating chatbots without coding is a growing trend that benefits greatly from proper integrations. By integrating messaging platforms such as WhatsApp or Facebook Messenger with customer services, businesses can automate responses to frequently asked questions, improving the customer experience and freeing up human resources for more complex tasks. These integrations allow chatbots to access databases and customer relationship management (CRM) systems, providing them with the information needed to deliver personalized responses.

In addition, integrating e-commerce platforms with digital marketing automation tools is essential to maximize online sales. By connecting inventory management systems and email marketing platforms, businesses can send automated emails to customers when a product is back in stock or when there are special offers. Not only does this improve the shopping experience, but it also boosts customer loyalty by keeping them informed and engaged.

Finally, creating no-code forms and surveys is another area where integrations can transform data collection. By integrating these tools with analytics applications, companies can gain valuable insights into customer satisfaction or product performance quickly and efficiently. These integrations allow users to automate data collection and analysis, making it easier to make informed, strategic decisions in business development and product improvement.

Best Practices for Integration

The integration of various tools and applications is essential to optimize processes and maximize efficiency in any automation strategy. To achieve a successful integration, it is vital to follow certain best practices that facilitate the flow of information and collaboration between platforms. These practices not only help avoid technical issues, but also allow users, with no programming experience, to implement effective and customized solutions.

One of the best practices is to clearly define the objectives of the integration. Before connecting different tools, it is essential to have a clear vision of what you want to achieve. This can include improving social media management, automating data collection, or facilitating communication between applications. By setting specific goals, you can select the right tools and configure integrations in a way that aligns with those goals.

In addition, it is advisable to use automation platforms that offer an intuitive interface and predefined integration options. Tools such as Zapier or Integromat allow you to connect applications without coding, making it easier to create automated workflows. These platforms usually have templates that can be adapted to the user's needs, saving time and effort in setting up complex integrations.

The documentation and support community are valuable resources when implementing integrations. Taking advantage of guides, tutorials, and forums can provide solutions to common problems and offer inspiration on how to optimize workflows. In addition, participating in online communities allows you to learn from the experience of other users and share effective practices that have worked in different contexts.

Finally, it's crucial to regularly test and adjust integrations. As business needs change or tools evolve, it's important to review and optimize integrations to ensure they remain effective. This proactive approach not only improves efficiency, but also helps identify new opportunities for automation and growth in the use of no-code tools.

Chapter 6

Social Media Management Automation

Scheduling of publications

Post scheduling is one of the most effective strategies for handling social media automatically and efficiently. Today, businesses and entrepreneurs are looking to maximize their online presence without having to spend hours managing their people on a daily basis. Thanks to various automation tools, it is possible to schedule content in advance, ensuring that posts are made at the optimal times to reach the desired audience. Not only does this save time, but it also allows for better planning of digital marketing campaigns.

When scheduling posts, it's essential to create a content calendar that reflects the brand's goals and key messages. This calendar should include important dates, promotions, product launches, and other relevant events. Automation tools make it possible not only to set posting schedules, but also to adapt content to different platforms, ensuring that each message is suitable for its respective channel. This is essential, as each social network has its own format and style of communication.

In addition, post scheduling makes it easy to integrate productivity tools that streamline workflow. Many of these platforms offer options to analyze the performance of scheduled posts, allowing for real-time strategic adjustments. For example, if a particular post generates more engagement, it's possible to replicate that type of content in future campaigns. This feedback is valuable for continuously improving your digital marketing strategy.

Automation isn't just limited to scheduling posts; It also includes developing chatbots and creating no-code forms that can interact with the audience. These tools make it possible to collect valuable information about users, which in turn helps to further personalize scheduled posts. Effective interaction with followers is key to increasing brand loyalty and fostering a sense of community around it.

Finally, it's important to remember that post scheduling is only one part of a larger automation strategy. Integrating e-commerce platforms and creating websites without the need for coding also play a crucial role in the user experience. By combining all these tools, a digital ecosystem can be built that not only automates social media management, but also boosts business growth significantly.

Metrics and Performance Analysis

Metrics and performance analysis is a critical part of social media management and process automation. In this context, it is crucial to understand how our strategies are performing and what data we can extract to continuously improve. By using automation tools, it is possible to collect and analyze data without the need for advanced technical knowledge. This allows anyone, regardless of skill level, to gain valuable insights into the effectiveness of their campaigns and audience interaction with their content.

The most relevant metrics to consider include engagement rate, post reach, and follower growth. These figures offer a clear view of how content resonates with the audience. For example, a high engagement rate may indicate that content is relevant and engaging, while a low reach suggests that the publishing strategy or type of content being shared needs to be adjusted. Automation tools allow you to constantly track these metrics, making it easier to identify patterns and trends.

Moreover, metrics analysis is not limited to social media alone, but can also be applied to various areas of digital marketing. For example, in building no-code mobile apps, it's critical to evaluate the performance of functionalities and user experience. Automation platforms can help collect feedback and usage data, allowing for continuous improvements in application development. This translates into a more efficient product that is aligned with user expectations.

The integration of productivity tools also plays an essential role in the analysis of metrics. By combining different platforms, such as project management systems and data analytics tools, a more complete view of performance can be obtained. Not only does this streamline workflow, but it also allows users to access detailed reports without the need for programming. This makes it easier to make informed decisions based on hard data.

Finally, chatbot development and business workflow automation are areas where metric analysis can make a big difference. By evaluating the effectiveness of a chatbot, for example, it is possible to identify the most common questions and areas that need improvement. This ensures that automation not only saves time, but also improves the user experience. In short, metrics and performance analysis is an essential tool that, combined with automation, allows anyone to optimize their processes without the need for technical knowledge.

Tools for automated management

In today's digital age, automation has become an essential tool for optimizing processes and improving efficiency in various areas. For those who do not have programming knowledge, there are multiple automated management tools that allow you to implement these solutions without the need to write a single line of code. Not only do these tools make it easier to automate routine tasks, but they also allow businesses and entrepreneurs to focus on more strategic aspects of their business.

One of the most relevant categories in this area is the automation of digital marketing processes. Platforms such as Zapier and Integromat allow different applications and services to be connected, facilitating the transfer of data between them. For example, you can automate the lead capture process by integrating web forms with email marketing tools, thus ensuring that each contact is managed efficiently, without manual intervention.

In addition, the creation of no-code mobile apps has gained popularity thanks to platforms such as Adalo and Glide. These tools allow any user to design and launch applications that suit their needs, without the need for technical knowledge. With customizable templates and built-in functionalities, it is possible to create innovative solutions that improve the user experience and optimize service management.

Social media management automation is another area where no-code tools shine. Apps like Buffer and Hootsuite allow you to schedule posts, analyze metrics, and manage multiple accounts from a single platform. Not only does this save time, but it also ensures a consistent presence on social media, which is critical for any brand's growth and visibility in the digital environment.

Finally, the integration of productivity tools also plays a crucial role in automating business workflows. Apps like Airtable and Notion make it easy to manage projects, collaborate as a team, and automate reporting and data analysis. These tools help businesses maintain an organized workflow, facilitating informed decision-making and improving collaboration across departments. In short, automated management is an indispensable resource for any person or company looking to optimize their processes without the need for technical knowledge.

Chapter 7

Development of Chatbots Without Programming

Types of chatbots and their usefulness

Chatbots are versatile tools that have become essential in the digital realm, facilitating interaction between companies and users. There are several types of chatbots, each designed to fulfill specific functions, which makes them strategic allies in the automation of processes. From handling simple queries to managing more complex tasks, chatbots optimize the customer experience and allow businesses to focus on higher-value activities.

One of the most common types is rule-based chatbots. These work by following a preset of instructions and responses. They are ideal for simple tasks, such as answering frequently asked questions or guiding users through a specific process, such as purchasing a product. Their implementation is simple and requires no programming knowledge, making them accessible to anyone interested in automating their customer service.

On the other hand, there are intelligent chatbots, which use artificial intelligence and machine learning to offer more personalized interactions. These chatbots can learn from conversations and adapt to the user's needs over time. They are particularly useful in digital marketing, as they can segment customers and offer personalized recommendations based on their behaviors and preferences, which increases the effectiveness of campaigns.

There are also voice chatbots, which allow users to interact through voice commands. This modality has gained popularity with the proliferation of virtual assistants such as Alexa and Google Assistant. Their usefulness lies in the convenience they offer, allowing users to perform tasks without the need to type, which improves accessibility and the overall user experience.

Finally, integration chatbots are those that connect with other tools and platforms, making it easier to automate business workflows. For example, they can be integrated with social media management systems, e-commerce platforms, or data analytics tools. Not only does this save time, but it also provides a more complete view of business performance, allowing informed decisions to be made based on real data. The diversity of chatbots available gives businesses the opportunity to choose the solution that best suits their needs, without the need for technical knowledge.

Platforms for creating chatbots

Platforms for creating chatbots have revolutionized the way businesses interact with their customers. These automated systems allow you to answer frequently asked questions, guide users in their purchasing decisions, and offer customer support efficiently. Through no-code tools, anyone can design a chatbot without the need for technical knowledge. This democratizes access to automation, making it easier for small businesses and entrepreneurs to benefit from this technology.

There are several platforms on the market that allow the creation of chatbots in an intuitive way. Some of the most popular ones influence Chatfuel, ManyChat, and Tars. These tools offer graphical interfaces that allow you to drag and drop elements, creating conversation flows in a simple way. In addition, many of them provide pre-designed templates that can be adapted to different industries, saving time and effort in the initial design. Thus, even those who have no previous programming experience can develop effective solutions.

The integration of chatbots in digital marketing has become essential to optimize contact with customers. Through automated strategies, it is possible to track leads, send purchase reminders, and offer personalized promotions. Not only do these platforms allow for the creation of chatbots, but they also often offer data analytics that help understand user behavior. This information is valuable for adjusting marketing strategies and improving the customer experience.

Enterprise workflow automation tools also benefit from the implementation of chatbots. By integrating these platforms with project management systems and CRM, companies can automate repetitive tasks, such as collecting data and sending reports. Not only does this save time, but it also reduces the chance of human error, improving operational efficiency. The creation of chatbots thus becomes a fundamental component for the digital transformation of any organization.

Finally, it is important to note that the creation of chatbots is not limited to large companies. Entrepreneurs and small businesses can take advantage of these tools to offer 24/7 customer service, improve their social media presence, and optimize communication with their customers. With accessible and easy-to-use platforms, process automation using chatbots is presented as a viable and effective solution for anyone interested in improving their business, without the need to be a technology expert.

Chatbot implementation and optimization

The implementation and optimization of chatbots has become an essential tool for companies looking to automate their customer service and digital marketing processes without the need for programming knowledge. Chatbots allow you to interact with users instantly, answering their questions and guiding them through different services, all automatically. Not only does this improve the user experience, but it also frees up time and resources so that human teams can focus on more complex and creative tasks.

To implement a chatbot, it is essential to clearly define the objectives to be achieved. This can include anything from customer support, where the chatbot answers frequently asked questions, to lead generation, where user data is collected for future campaigns. Using no-code platforms facilitates this process, as they offer intuitive interfaces that allow you to design and program the chatbot's behavior without the need to write code. Tools such as Chatfuel or ManyChat are examples of platforms that allow chatbots to be created in an accessible and efficient way.

Once the chatbot is up and running, constant optimization is crucial to ensure its effectiveness. This involves analyzing user interactions, identifying patterns, and adjusting the chatbot's responses to improve its performance. Metrics to consider include response rate, user satisfaction, and query resolution time. By using analytics tools and metrics, you can get a clear view of how the chatbot is performing and what areas require improvement.

In addition, it is essential to integrate the chatbot with other productivity tools and e-commerce platforms. This will allow the chatbot to not only answer questions, but also perform specific actions, such as processing orders or sending reminders. Integration with platforms such as Shopify or Mailchimp can increase the chatbot's functionality, turning it into a virtual assistant that maximizes the efficiency of business workflows.

Finally, creating forms and surveys through the chatbot can be a valuable strategy for gathering information from users. This data is essential to adjust marketing strategies and improve the offer of products or services. By incorporating automation into these processes, companies can gain valuable insights quickly and effectively, allowing them to quickly adapt to market needs. In summary, the implementation and optimization of chatbots is a fundamental step towards process automation, providing both companies and users with a smoother and more efficient experience.

Chapter 8

Business Workflow Automation

Identification of processes susceptible to automation

Identifying processes susceptible to automation is a critical step for anyone who wants to optimize their time and resources without the need for advanced technical knowledge. In the context of no-code automation, it's essential to recognize which of your day-to-day tasks can benefit from tools that simplify their execution. This process begins with a detailed analysis of routine activities that consume time and effort, thus allowing you to prioritize the implementation of automated solutions.

A good place to start is to examine digital marketing processes, where automation can ease the burden of tasks such as scheduling social media posts and managing email campaigns. For example, tools like Hootsuite or Mailchimp allow users to schedule content and segment audiences without requiring programming knowledge. By identifying these areas, greater efficiency in reaching and interacting with the target audience can be achieved.

Creating forms and surveys is another area that lends itself to automation. Platforms such as Google Forms or Typeform allow users to design custom forms to collect information without the need for coding. Identifying the need to obtain customer data or conduct satisfaction surveys can be the first step towards implementing these resources, facilitating further analysis of the information collected.

In addition, automating business workflows has become a key aspect of improving productivity. Tools such as Zapier or Integromat can integrate various applications and automate tasks between them, such as data synchronization between a CRM and an e-commerce platform. By identifying friction points in these flows, companies can avoid duplication of effort and ensure that information flows smoothly.

Finally, the development of no-code chatbots represents a growing trend in customer service automation. Identifying common FAQs or requests can guide the creation of a chatbot that manages these interactions efficiently. Not only does this save time, but it also improves the customer experience, allowing staff to focus on more complex tasks. In short, recognizing and prioritizing processes susceptible to automation is a strategy that can transform the way we work, making the optimization of everyday tasks more accessible.

Workflow automation tools

Workflow automation tools have revolutionized the way businesses and individuals manage their daily tasks. These tools allow you to optimize processes, saving time and resources, without the need for advanced programming knowledge. In a world where efficiency is key, these no-code solutions have become indispensable allies for those who want to improve their operations without complicating themselves with code.

One of the areas where automation has a noticeable impact is in digital marketing. Tools such as Zapier or Integromat allow you to connect applications and create automatic workflows that manage everything from sending emails to publishing content on social networks. This means that, for example, every time a new article is published on a blog, it can be automatically shared on the chosen social platforms, thus increasing visibility without the need for manual intervention.

When it comes to creating mobile apps, there are platforms like Adalo or Glide that allow users to develop apps without writing a single line of code. These tools offer templates and components that can be easily customized, making it easy for anyone, no matter their level of technical expertise, to launch their own app. Not only does this democratize access to technology, but it also fosters innovation by allowing ideas that might previously be left in the air to materialize.

Integrating productivity tools is another crucial aspect of workflow automation. Apps like Trello or Asana can be combined with other management and communication tools, allowing tasks to be automatically assigned and progress to be recorded effortlessly.

This is especially useful in collaborative environments, where coordination between teams can be a challenge. With these integrations, project management becomes more seamless and effective.

Finally, automating reporting and data analysis is a vital component of making informed decisions. Tools like Google Data Studio allow you to create visual reports that are automatically updated from a variety of data sources. This means that instead of spending hours manually gathering information, users can access real-time analytics that will help them better understand how their strategies are performing. In short, workflow automation tools are an accessible and effective solution for those looking to improve their productivity and efficiency without the need for programming knowledge. Process Documentation and Tracking

Documentation and process tracking are critical to ensuring success in automating tasks within any digital marketing strategy. In an environment where social media and digital platforms play a crucial role, having a clear and accessible record of each of the steps that are carried out is vital. This not only allows for better organization, but also makes it easier to identify areas for improvement and optimize resources. Proper documentation helps companies keep tabs on their actions and understand the impact of each process on their overall goals.

One of the most important aspects of process documentation is the creation of manuals or guides that detail each step of the workflow.

This includes everything from initial planning to execution and evaluation of results. By using no-code tools, it is possible to design forms, surveys, and workflows that are easily integrated into documentation. These tools allow anyone, without the need for technical knowledge, to contribute to the creation of a more efficient and organized work environment.

Process tracking doesn't just involve observing what has been done, but also analyzing results and collecting relevant data. This can be achieved through report automation, which allows for continuous, real-time analytics to be generated. By integrating e-commerce platforms and productivity tools, businesses can gain a clear view of their performance metrics, making it easier to make informed decisions. This approach helps identify patterns and trends that might go unnoticed in manual analysis.

In addition, social media management benefits greatly from good documentation and tracking. By establishing a publication schedule and recording the interactions and results of each post, the effectiveness of the strategies implemented can be evaluated. Automation tools make it possible to schedule content and track audience engagement, providing valuable insights into follower preferences and behaviors. This information can be used to adjust tactics and maximize the impact of future campaigns.

Finally, it is important to note that documentation and process monitoring are not static tasks. They should be reviewed and updated regularly to reflect changes in strategies or the digital environment. Automating business workflows allows these adjustments to be made in an agile and efficient way. By integrating different tools and platforms, an ecosystem can be created where information flows frictionlessly, facilitating a more fluid experience for both work teams and customers. In this way, documentation and monitoring become key allies in the search for excellence in process automation.

Chapter 9

Creating No-Code Forms and Surveys

Tools for Forms and Surveys

Having effective tools for creating forms and surveys is critical to any automation strategy. These tools allow users to collect valuable data easily and without the need for technical knowledge. There are multiple platforms that offer no-code solutions, making it easy to create custom forms and interactive surveys that can be easily integrated into websites and social media.

One of the most popular tools in this area is Google Forms, which allows users to design forms quickly and for free. Its intuitive interface makes it easy to add different types of questions, from multiple choice to rating scales. In addition, the collected data is automatically stored in Google Sheets, making it simple to analyze and visualize the information obtained. This integration is ideal for those looking for a practical and accessible solution.

Another prominent option is Typeform, which focuses on the user experience by offering visually appealing and dynamic surveys and forms. Through its platform, users can create interactive forms that keep the respondent's attention and increase response rates. In addition, Typeform allows integration with various automation tools, such as Zapier, making it easy to flow information between applications without the need for programming.

For those looking for a more comprehensive option, JotForm comes across as a robust tool that offers a wide range of templates and customization options. This platform allows you not only to create forms and surveys, but also to manage payments and collect customer information efficiently. With its drag-and-drop functionality, JotForm is ideal for those who want to create complex forms without technical complications.

Finally, it is important to mention the relevance of automation in the management of data obtained through forms and surveys. Tools such as Airtable and Google Data Studio allow you to analyze and visualize information effectively, transforming raw data into valuable insights for decision-making. The integration of these tools not only optimizes the data collection process, but also improves efficiency in analyzing and presenting results, thus empowering any digital marketing and process automation strategy.

Best Practices for Data Collection

Data collection is a fundamental process in any automation strategy, especially in the realm of digital marketing and social media management. To maximize the effectiveness of this process, it is crucial to follow certain best practices that ensure the quality and relevance of the information collected. One of the first recommendations is to clearly define the objectives of data collection. This involves identifying what kind of information is needed to make informed decisions and how this data aligns with the overall business goals.

Once the objectives have been established, it is important to select the right tools for data collection. There are several no-code platforms that make it easy to create forms and surveys intuitively. When choosing a tool, consider ease of use, the ability to integrate with other apps you already use, and the ability to customize questions to suit your needs. Platforms like Google Forms or Typeform are great options to get started, as they allow you to collect data effectively without the need for advanced technical knowledge.

In addition, it is essential to ensure the quality of the data collected. This can be achieved by implementing validation and verification methods in the collection process. For example, when creating forms, be sure to include required fields and apply specific formatting for certain types of information, such as emails or phone numbers. Not only does this improve data accuracy, but it also reduces the time spent cleaning up information after collection.

Another best practice is data segmentation. By classifying information based on different criteria, such as demographics, behavior, or preferences, you can gain more detailed and useful insights. Segmentation allows you to personalize marketing and communication strategies, thus optimizing the performance of your campaigns. Automation tools can help manage this segmentation efficiently, allowing the data to be easily accessible and usable for future actions.

Finally, it is important to periodically review and analyze the data collected. Establishing a timeline for evaluating information will allow you to identify trends, opportunities for improvement, and areas that need attention. Use analytics tools that easily integrate data to generate clear and concise reports. This way, you'll be able to adjust your strategies based on the insights gained, ensuring that your approach to process automation remains effective and relevant in an ever-changing digital environment.

Analysis of results obtained

In the analysis of the results obtained, it is essential to evaluate the impact of the automation strategies implemented in the various niches we cover. Automating digital marketing processes, for example, has proven to be a powerful tool for increasing efficiency and reducing response times. Through the use of no-code platforms, users have been able to create personalized campaigns that not only optimize reach, but also allow for comprehensive tracking of key metrics, facilitating informed decision-making.

Likewise, the creation of no-code mobile apps has revolutionized the way entrepreneurs and small businesses interact with their customers. When analyzing the results obtained, a significant increase in user satisfaction is observed, thanks to the ease of access and customization that these applications offer. No-code tools allow for rapid iteration, which means businesses can quickly adapt to changing market needs without relying on third-party developers.

Regarding the automation of social media management, the results indicate that companies that have adopted these strategies have achieved a notable increase in their *engagement* and customer loyalty. The integration of productivity tools has made it easier to schedule posts and interact in real-time, resulting in a more active and relevant online presence. This analysis reveals that by automating repetitive tasks, teams can focus on creating valuable content, which in turn boosts brand image.

The development of no-code chatbots has also been an area of great impact. When evaluating the results, it is evident that these virtual assistants not only improve customer service, but also allow valuable data to be collected on user preferences and behaviors. This information is crucial for adjusting strategies and delivering a more personalized service, which in the long run translates into increased conversions and customer loyalty.

Finally, automating reporting and data analytics has allowed companies to gain a clearer view of their performance. The integration of e-commerce platforms and the creation of no-code forms and surveys have made it easier to collect key information. The results obtained show that companies that use these tools not only save time, but can also identify trends and opportunities that might have otherwise gone unnoticed. Together, these analyses demonstrate the transformative potential of automation in various aspects of the business.

Chapter 10

Reporting Automation and Data Analysis

No-code data analysis tools

No-code data analysis tools have revolutionized the way businesses and professionals manage and process information. These solutions allow users, without technical expertise, to effectively extract, visualize, and analyze data. By eliminating the need to write code, access to data intelligence is democratized, empowering anyone to make informed decisions based on hard data. This is especially valuable in the realm of digital marketing and social media management, where the ability to analyze the performance of campaigns and posts can make the difference between success and failure.

One of the most popular tools in this area is Google Data Studio. This platform allows users to create interactive reports and engaging visualizations from various data sources. Its intuitive interface makes it easy to customize *dashboards*, allowing marketers to track key metrics without the need for programming skills. In addition, its integration with other Google tools, such as Google Analytics and Google Ads, offers a complete view of the performance of digital strategies.

Another prominent option is Tableau Public, which, while designed for more advanced users, also offers accessible functionality for those who are not code-savvy. With Tableau, users can connect their data and generate impactful visualizations that make it easier to understand trends and patterns. This tool is especially useful for report automation, as it allows data to be updated in real-time, saving time and effort in report preparation.

For those interested in creating forms and surveys, platforms like Typeform and Google Forms come across as no-code solutions that are easy to use and highly effective. Not only do these tools make it easy to collect data, but they also offer built-in analysis options that help interpret the results. This is essential for optimizing marketing strategies and better understanding the needs and preferences of the target audience.

Finally, business workflow automation can benefit greatly from tools like Zapier and Integromat. These platforms allow users to integrate different applications and automate repetitive tasks without the need for programming. By connecting productivity tools, such as spreadsheets and e-commerce platforms, it is easier to analyze data and make decisions quickly and based on up-to-date information. In summary, no-code data analytics tools are critical for anyone looking to streamline their processes and make informed decisions in today's digital environment.

Automated reporting

Automated reporting has become an essential tool for businesses looking to optimize their performance and make informed decisions. In the context of social media and digital marketing, reports allow professionals to analyze the impact of their strategies and adjust their tactics based on hard data. Thanks to no-code tools and process automation, anyone can generate detailed and visual reports without the need for advanced technical knowledge.

To start creating automated reports, it's critical to identify which metrics are relevant to your business. These metrics can include follower growth, post engagement, ad campaign conversion rates, and other key performance indicators (KPIs). Once the metrics have been defined, platforms such as Google Data Studio, Airtable, or Zapier can be used to collect and visualize this data in a simple way. These tools allow you to integrate various sources of information, facilitating the creation of a complete and accurate report.

Automating the reporting process not only saves time, but also minimizes the risk of human error. By scheduling data collection and reporting at regular intervals, users can receive up-to-date analytics without having to manually track them. This is especially useful for businesses that run multiple social media accounts or run marketing campaigns on various platforms. Consistency in reporting allows marketing teams to react quickly to changes in performance.

In addition, customization is key when generating automated reports. No-code tools allow you to tailor the design and structure of reports to the specific needs of the user or client. Graphs, tables, and summaries can be included to facilitate the understanding of the data. By offering visually appealing and easy-to-interpret reports, the communication of results to stakeholders is improved, which can influence strategic decision-making.

Finally, automated reporting brings significant value to the data analysis process. By reducing manual workload and providing real-time insights, businesses can focus on implementing data-driven strategies instead of spending time gathering information. With the use of the right tools and a clear focus on relevant metrics, anyone can benefit from report automation, thereby improving their social media management and the performance of their digital marketing campaigns. Data interpretation and decision-making.

Data interpretation is a fundamental process in decision-making, especially in the field of social networks and process automation. In a world where information is constantly flowing, knowing how to analyze and understand data becomes an essential skill for anyone interested in optimizing their online presence. The ability to interpret data allows you to identify trends, user behaviors, and areas for improvement, resulting in more informed and effective decisions.

One of the main benefits of automation in this context is the ease with which data can be collected and analyzed. No-code tools allow users to set up systems that collect information automatically, whether through forms, surveys, or social media interactions. These tools offer *visual dashboards and reports that simplify the understanding of information, making it easier to identify patterns and generate valuable insights without the need for advanced programming knowledge.*

Data-driven decision-making is supported by the integration of different platforms and tools. For example, by connecting a social media management system with a data analytics tool, you can get a holistic view of how campaigns and posts are performing. This integration not only saves time, but also allows adjustments to be made in real-time, maximizing the impact of digital marketing strategies. Automating these processes ensures that information is always up-to-date and available for analysis.

In addition, the development of chatbots and automated workflows allows businesses to respond quickly to their customers' needs. By collecting data on user interactions, adjustments can be made to marketing strategies, thereby improving the customer experience and increasing the conversion rate. The ability to interpret and act on this data is crucial for any business looking to stand out in an increasingly competitive and digital market.

Finally, automating reporting and data analysis not only improves decision-making, but also frees up time for professionals to focus on strategic tasks. By eliminating the manual workload associated with data collection and analysis, businesses can focus on creativity and innovation. In an environment where adaptability is key, having automated processes that facilitate the interpretation of data becomes a significant competitive advantage for any organization looking to thrive in the digital realm.

Chapter 11

E-Commerce Platform Integration

Tools for e-commerce management

E-commerce management has evolved significantly, and the tools available to facilitate this task are more accessible than ever. For those who want to automate sales processes without the need for programming knowledge, there are several platforms that allow you to integrate and optimize every aspect of an online business. These tools not only simplify management, but also enhance the efficiency and effectiveness of business operations.

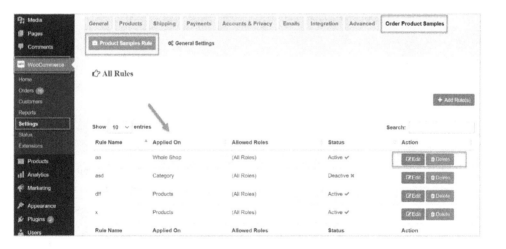

One of the most popular tools in e-commerce management is Shopify. This platform offers complete solutions for creating and managing online stores without writing code. With an intuitive interface, it allows users to customize their store, manage inventory, and process payments easily. In addition, Shopify has a wide variety of applications that can be integrated to automate tasks such as sending emails to customers, social media management, and sales analytics, thus facilitating the automation of digital marketing processes.

Another prominent option is WooCommerce, a WordPress plugin that transforms any website into an online store. This tool is ideal for those who are already familiar with the WordPress ecosystem. WooCommerce allows for product creation, reservation management, and order tracking, all without the need for programming. Its flexibility allows you to integrate various applications that help improve the user experience and optimize business management, from chatbots for customer service to data analysis tools.

For those interested in creating forms and surveys, Google Forms is presented as a simple and effective tool. It allows you to capture customer information quickly and without complications. By integrating Google Forms with automation tools like Zapier, it is possible to automatically send responses to other platforms, making it easier to manage data and generate reports. This integration is key to maintaining an organized and efficient workflow in an e-commerce environment.

Finally, integrating e-commerce platforms with social networks is essential to maximize the reach of a business. Tools such as Hootsuite or Buffer allow you to schedule posts on different social networks, which ensures a constant and effective online presence. These platforms also offer detailed analytics on the performance of each publication, allowing you to adjust marketing strategies based on audience behavior. Thus, automation in social media management becomes an essential ally for the success of any online store.

Sales Process Automation

Automating sales processes has become a key strategy for companies looking to optimize their performance and make more efficient use of their resources. Through automation tools, it is possible to manage repetitive and tedious tasks, allowing sales teams to focus on what really matters: closing sales and building strong customer relationships. The good news is that there are solutions today that don't require programming knowledge, making these tools accessible to anyone interested in improving their business.

One of the main advantages of sales process automation is the ability to personalize the customer experience. By integrating e-commerce platforms with customer relationship management (CRM) systems, a more agile service can be offered and adapted to the needs of each user. For example, automation tools allow you to send personalized emails, segment audiences, and create targeted marketing campaigns, all without writing a single line of code. Not only does this improve customer satisfaction, but it also increases conversion rates.

In addition, the automation of sales processes facilitates data analysis. Automation platforms can collect and analyze insights into customer behavior, allowing businesses to make informed decisions based on real data. From identifying buying patterns to evaluating the effectiveness of marketing campaigns, these tools offer a clear view of business performance. Thus, entrepreneurs can adjust their strategies and optimize their sales efforts without technical complications.

Chatbot building is another area where automation has transformed the way sales are made. These virtual assistants, which can be implemented without programming knowledge, allow you to interact with customers in real time, answer frequently asked questions and guide users through the purchase process. By reducing the workload of the sales team and improving customer service, chatbots help businesses maintain constant and effective communication, which translates into increased sales.

Finally, automating business workflows and integrating various productivity tools are critical to achieving a more efficient sales process. By connecting applications and platforms through automation tools, the entire sales cycle can be managed from one place. Not only does this save time, but it also minimizes errors and improves collaboration between teams. In short, sales process automation is an accessible and effective strategy that can revolutionize the way companies operate, regardless of their size or sector.

Best Practices for Platform Integration

Best practices for platform integration are critical to optimizing processes and ensuring that all tools used work together and efficiently. In an environment where automation is booming, it's crucial to understand how to connect different applications and services without the need for programming skills. Not only does this save time, but it also minimizes errors and improves overall productivity. By following these practices, anyone interested in process automation can benefit greatly.

First, it is essential to identify the platforms that will be used in the integration process. This influences digital marketing tools, social media management services, form builders, and productivity apps. By knowing the functionalities and features of each platform, it is easier to create workflows that take full advantage of the capabilities of each tool. Prior research on the available integrations and how they can interact is a crucial step that should not be overlooked.

Once the platforms have been selected, the next step is to define the goals of the integration. This involves establishing which processes you want to automate and how you expect these integrations to improve efficiency. For example, if the goal is to automate social media management, it's critical to determine which posts should be scheduled, what metrics are important, and how performance data can be collected. Having clarity on the objectives will help create an action plan that guides the integration process.

Using no-code tools is another best practice to consider. These tools allow users to create integrations and automations without the need for advanced technical knowledge. There are several platforms that offer easy-to-use solutions for connecting applications, such as Zapier or Integromat. By using these tools, platform integration can be simplified, making workflow automation accessible to everyone, regardless of their level of technical expertise.

Finally, it is important to monitor and analyse the results obtained after integration. This includes monitoring the performance of automated processes and making adjustments as needed to optimize results. Constant feedback is key to improving efficiency and adapting to changing business needs. By applying these best practices in platform integration, anyone can maximize the benefits of automation and achieve effective control over their processes without the need for programming.

Chapter 12

Website Development Without Coding

Platforms for website creation

Nowadays, creating a website has become an accessible task for anyone, even those who don't have technical or programming skills. There are a number of platforms specifically designed to simplify this process, allowing users to build attractive and functional websites in just a few steps. Not only do these tools eliminate the need to learn programming languages, but they also offer customizable templates and layouts that cater to different needs and styles.

One of the most popular platforms is WordPress, which offers a user-friendly interface and a wide variety of themes and plugins. With WordPress, users can create everything from personal blogs to corporate websites without writing a single line of code. In addition, its active community provides support and resources that make the creation process even easier. WordPress' flexibility makes it an ideal choice for those who want to automate certain processes by integrating digital marketing and social media management tools.

Another prominent option is Wix, which allows users to drag and drop elements to build their websites. With a focus on simplicity, Wix offers pre-built templates that can be easily customized. Its visual editor is intuitive, making it easy to create web pages even for beginners. In addition, Wix includes SEO and marketing tools that help optimize the site's visibility in search engines, which is essential for any automation strategy in the digital realm.

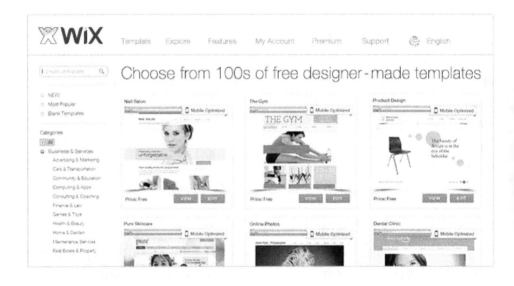

Shopify is a platform specially designed for those who want to set up an online store. Through Shopify, users can create an eCommerce website without requiring technical expertise. The platform allows the integration of inventory management, payment processing, and data analysis tools, resulting in a comprehensive solution for process automation in digital commerce. Additionally, Shopify offers the ability to customize the store's layout, ensuring that each business has its own online identity.

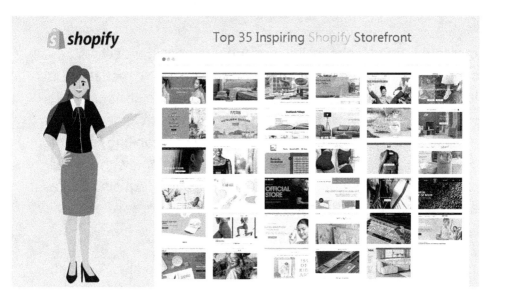

Finally, tools like Squarespace and Weebly are also worth mentioning. These platforms combine sleek design with ease of use, allowing users to create visually appealing websites without complications. Squarespace is known for its modern designs, ideal for portfolios and presentation sites. Meanwhile, Weebly offers e-commerce features and a simple interface, making it a viable option for small businesses. In short, website creation platforms have democratized access to online presence, facilitating process automation and freeing users from the need for advanced technical knowledge.

Essential elements for a good website

To create a good website, it is essential to consider several essential elements that not only improve the user experience but also optimize process automation. First of all, the structure and design must be intuitive. A well-organized website allows visitors to navigate easily, finding the information they are looking for without complications. Using a clean, modern design, along with a clear hierarchy of information, not only engages users, but also makes it easier to implement automation tools that can improve efficiency.

Another crucial aspect is the loading speed of the site. A website that loads quickly not only provides a better user experience, but also affects search engine rankings. There are a variety of no-code tools that allow you to optimize images and files, as well as configure the site's cache, which is essential for keeping visitors on the page and reducing the bounce rate. Automation in this regard can be very beneficial, as it allows continuous adjustments to be made based on the performance of the site.

Mobile compatibility is another indispensable element today. With the increased use of mobile devices to access the internet, it is crucial that the website looks and functions perfectly on smaller screens. Using no-code website builder platforms that offer responsive designs makes this task easier. In addition, the integration of analytics tools can help monitor user behavior on mobile devices, allowing automatic adjustments to be made according to their preferences.

Website security should not be overlooked. Implementing security measures such as SSL certificates and authentication options can protect both the site and its users. There are tools that allow you to automate security management, such as updating plugins and performing regular backups. Not only does this provide peace of mind for the site owners, but it also fosters trust among visitors.

Finally, content is the king of any website. It is essential to offer relevant and up-to-date information that appeals to the target audience. Automation can play an important role here, making it easier to schedule blog posts or manage social media that drive traffic to the site. In addition, using no-code forms and surveys allows you to collect valuable user data, which can help personalize content and improve audience interaction. A good website is not only attractive and functional, but also a dynamic resource that can adapt to the changing needs of users.

Automated Website Optimization and Maintenance

Automated website optimization and maintenance is a crucial aspect of ensuring that these platforms work efficiently and meet business goals. In an ever-changing digital environment, it's vital that websites are kept up-to-date and optimized to improve the user experience and maximize conversion. This involves not only creating relevant content, but also implementing automation tools that make it easier to manage and monitor the site.

One of the main strategies for optimizing an automated website is the use of analytics tools. These tools allow you to measure site performance, identify areas for improvement, and adjust your content strategy accordingly. For example, platforms like Google Analytics provide valuable insights into user behavior, which can help adjust the site's design and functionality to improve the visitor experience. Reporting automation can also simplify data collection, allowing site owners to focus on analysis and data-driven decision-making.

Regular site maintenance is also essential. This includes updating plugins, checking broken links, and optimizing load time. Automation tools can schedule these tasks, ensuring they are done in a timely and efficient manner. Additionally, maintaining an automated website should include reviewing content to maintain its relevance and freshness, which is key for SEO and user retention.

The integration of e-commerce platforms and productivity tools also plays an important role in website optimization and maintenance. Automating processes such as inventory management and customer support through chatbots can significantly improve operational efficiency. These integrations allow site owners to focus on growth strategies, while routine tasks are managed automatically.

Finally, creating no-code forms and surveys can be a great way to gather feedback from users, which in turn can guide future site optimizations. Automating the collection and analysis of this data makes it possible to identify trends and areas for improvement, ensuring that the website not only stays operational, but also evolves to meet the needs of its audience. With these strategies, users can manage their websites effectively, without the need for advanced technical knowledge.

Chapter 13

Future of No-Code Automation

Emerging Trends in Automation

Automation is undergoing significant evolution in various industries, driven by the need to optimize processes and improve efficiency. One of the emerging trends in this area is the rise of no-code tools, which allow users to create applications and automate processes without the need for programming knowledge. These platforms have democratized access to technology, allowing anyone, regardless of their technical background, to develop customized solutions that are tailored to their specific needs.

In the field of digital marketing, automation is becoming an essential component for businesses looking to maximize their reach and effectiveness. Tools that integrate social media management, emailing, and data analytics are enabling marketers to run more consistent and effective campaigns. Not only does this approach save time, but it also ensures that strategies are implemented more accurately, adjusting tactics in real-time based on consumer behavior.

Creating chatbots without coding is another trend that is revolutionizing the way businesses interact with their customers.

These automated systems can provide 24-hour customer support, solve common problems, and guide users through complex processes. With the advancement of artificial intelligence, chatbots are becoming increasingly sophisticated, offering personalized responses and improving the user experience without requiring human intervention.

The integration of productivity tools is also on the rise, making it easier to connect between different platforms and applications. This allows businesses to automate entire workflows, from project management to sales tracking. By consolidating data and processes in one place, organizations can optimize their operational performance and reduce the chance of human error. The ability to automatically generate reports and data analysis provides businesses with a clearer view of their performance and areas for improvement.

Finally, creating no-code forms and surveys is simplifying data collection and customer feedback. These tools allow businesses to design custom forms that can be easily integrated into their websites or social media. By automating data collection and analysis, businesses can make more informed and faster decisions. Together, these emerging trends in automation are transforming the way businesses operate, making them more agile and competitive in an ever-changing marketplace.

The impact of artificial intelligence

The impact of artificial intelligence in the field of process automation is profound and transformative. Today, artificial intelligence (AI) allows businesses and individuals to optimize their daily tasks, from managing social media to creating mobile apps without the need for coding skills. This technology provides tools that simplify automation, making solutions that previously required advanced technical expertise accessible. Thus, AI becomes a fundamental ally for those who seek to improve their productivity and efficiency.

One of the highlights of artificial intelligence is its ability to analyze large volumes of data in real-time. This is especially relevant in digital marketing, where AI can identify patterns of consumer behavior and offer personalized recommendations. By integrating these smart tools into marketing strategies, businesses can automate their campaigns and optimize their audience segmentation, resulting in a higher return on investment. AI-based automation therefore allows for more effective resource management and a more strategic approach to customer communication.

The creation of chatbots is another clear example of how artificial intelligence is revolutionizing the way companies interact with their customers. These virtual assistants can be programmed to answer frequently asked questions, manage reservations, or even make sales, all without human intervention. Not only does this save time and resources, but it also improves the user experience by providing quick and efficient responses. In addition, the implementation of chatbots does not require programming knowledge, which democratizes their use and allows more entrepreneurs and small businesses to benefit from this technology.

The automation of business workflows has also been driven by artificial intelligence. Tools that integrate different platforms and services allow companies to automate processes that were previously manual and tedious. For example, the integration of productivity tools and ecommerce platforms makes it easy to manage inventory, generate reports, and analyze data, all automatically. This frees work teams from repetitive tasks and allows them to focus on activities that require creativity and innovation.

In conclusion, the impact of artificial intelligence on process automation is undeniable and has opened up endless possibilities for those who want to improve their efficiency without the need for programming. From creating forms and surveys to developing websites, AI offers solutions that simplify and streamline daily work. As this technology continues to evolve, it is critical for both individuals and businesses to stay informed and leverage the tools available to them to stay competitive in an increasingly automated world.

Preparing for the Future of Automated Business

Preparing for the future of automated business involves understanding how technology can transform the way we operate. In a world where efficiency and speed are crucial, automation becomes an essential tool for any type of company, regardless of its size. For those who do not have programming skills, no-code solutions offer a gateway to this new paradigm, allowing anyone to implement automated processes in their businesses without having to write a single line of code.

One of the highlights of automation is its ability to streamline digital marketing processes.

Tools like email autoresponders and social media management platforms make it possible to schedule posts and segment audiences effectively. This not only saves time, but also improves the quality of communication with customers. Marketing automation allows businesses to focus on creativity and strategy, while repetitive tasks are managed automatically.

Creating no-code mobile apps is another area where automation is revolutionizing the business landscape. There are platforms that allow users to design and launch applications tailored to their needs without requiring technical knowledge. This is especially useful for entrepreneurs who want to offer innovative services without the traditional development costs and complications. With automation, any idea can be turned into a functional application in record time.

Integrating productivity tools is key to maximizing business efficiency. By automating workflows, companies can link different platforms and applications to work together. For example, a business can integrate its customer management system with its e-commerce platform to provide real-time updates on order status. Not only do these integrations improve the customer experience, but they also allow for smoother management of internal resources.

Finally, the automation of social media management and the creation of chatbots without programming are trends that cannot be ignored. These tools allow businesses to interact with their customers more efficiently, answer frequently asked questions, and maintain an active online presence. As the business environment continues to evolve, those who prepare to adopt these automated technologies will be better positioned to meet the challenges of the future and take advantage of the opportunities that arise.

Some businesses that could disappear

According to what we have seen in the book, some businesses will tend to disappear, or at least, to transform completely. No-code, artificial intelligence and automation are here to stay.

It's important to note that automation generally transforms jobs rather than eliminating them entirely. New roles and opportunities related to the management and supervision of automated systems will emerge and above all human skills such as creativity, empathy and strategic thinking will continue to be valuable. Perhaps, now, much more.

Services that require a high level of personalization and human contact will likely persist and those that need adaptation and continuous learning will be key to staying relevant.

Perhaps and at the risk of being wrong, the most vulnerable services will be these, although time, and not too far away, will prove me right.

Traditional Customer Service

      Basic Call Centers

      Top-notch support services

      Management of routine consultations

Administrative and processing jobs

      Data Entry

      Invoice processing

      Basic transcription

      Routine documentation management

Basic financial services

     Basic accounting

     Simple payroll management

     Basic Financial Analysis

     Routine banking services

Basic Translation Services

     Translation of simple texts

     Basic Location

     Single subtitling

Basic Design Services

     Simple logo design

     Creating Basic Banners

     Basic Photo Editing

Chapter 14

Conclusions and Notes

Conclusions

The no-code world has revolutionized the way we automate processes, democratizing technology and allowing professionals from various fields to create solutions without the need for in-depth technical knowledge.

Key takeaways from the book: No-code automation has proven especially valuable in:

- Optimizing Business Workflows
- Integration of different tools and platforms
- Reduction of repetitive tasks
- Improved process accuracy and consistency
- Significant time and resource savings

Proven Benefits

The case studies presented showed average time savings of 60-80% in administrative tasks and a significant reduction in human errors. Companies that implemented no-code solutions reported improvements in both employee and customer satisfaction.

Looking to the future

The continuous evolution of no-code tools suggests a future where automation will become increasingly accessible. Platforms will continue to expand their capabilities, enabling more complex and sophisticated automations without the need for code.

Recommendations to get started:

1. Identify repetitive processes in your organization
2. Evaluate the no-code tools available according to your specific needs
3. Start with small, scalable projects
4. Document and measure automation results
5. Maintain a mindset of continuous improvement

Tools mentioned

Workflow Automation

- Zapier (zapier.com): Connect different applications and automate workflows between them. Ideal for automating repetitive tasks between apps without code.
- Make/Integromat (make.com): Similar to Zapier but with a more visual interface. It allows you to create complex automation scenarios between applications.
- n8n (n8n.io): Open source alternative for workflow automation. It can be installed locally or used in the cloud.

Chatbots

- Chatfuel (chatfuel.com): Create chatbots for Facebook Messenger without coding. Focused on customer service and sales.
- ManyChat (manychat.com): Platform for creating conversational chatbots. Specialized in marketing and engagement in social networks.

Social Media Management

- Buffer (buffer.com): Schedule and analyze social media posts. Ideal for managing multiple networks from one place.
- Hootsuite (hootsuite.com): Complete platform for managing social networks, scheduling content and analyzing results.

Web creation

- WordPress (wordpress.com): Content management system for creating websites and blogs. Very versatile and with a large number of plugins.
- Wix (wix.com): Website builder with drag & drop system. Ideal for beginners due to its ease of use.
- Shopify (shopify.com): Specific platform for creating online stores. Includes inventory management and payments.
- Squarespace (squarespace.com): Platform for creating websites with elegant designs. Focused on portfolios and visual sites.
- Weebly (weebly.com): Simple website builder with basic ecommerce functionalities.

Databases and productivity

- Airtable (airtable.com): Combines spreadsheet and database functionalities. Ideal for project management and collaboration.
- Google Forms (forms.google.com): Create forms and surveys easily. Integrates with other Google tools.
- Typeform (typeform.com): Create interactive forms and surveys with an attractive design. Focused on user experience.
- JotForm (jotform.com): Complete platform for creating custom forms and managing responses.

From the Author

Thank you very much for reading this book.

I hope it has helped you find the number of tools we have at our disposal to carry out the usual daily tasks.

If you focus it well, you could spend more time making your work more enjoyable, much less monotonous and much more productive.

www.ingramcontent.com/pod-product-compliance
Lightning Source LLC
LaVergne TN
LVHW051709050326
832903LV00032B/4088

This book lets you discover how to automate your social media and digital marketing processes without any programming. This practical guide teaches you how to discover no-code tools to optimize your online presence and multiply your productivity.

Are you looking for ways to manage your daily work, your social media, more efficiently? This book shows you many tools to:

- Automate content publishing on multiple platforms
- Create effective chatbots without technical knowledge
- Implement automated email marketing strategies
- Develop mobile applications without writing code
- Integrate e-commerce and productivity tools
- Analyze data and generate automatic reports
- Optimize your online sales processes

ISBN 9798307105368

9 798307 105368